Goodword

Arabic

Picture Dictionary

For Kids

GOODWORD BOOKS

Written by: Saniyasnain Khan
Arabic Translation: Prof. Tayyeb Abu Sin
Illustrated by: Gurmeet
Art Editor: Mateen Ahmad
Designed by: Amar Nath Chatterjee

First published 2014
© Goodword Books 2014

Goodword Books
1, Nizamuddin West Market, New Delhi-110 013
Tel. +9111-4182-7083, Mob. +91-8588822672
email: info@goodwordbooks.com
www.goodwordbooks.com

Goodword Books, Chennai
82/324, Triplicane High Road, Chennai-600005
Mob. +91-9790853944

Islamic Vision Ltd.
434 Coventry Road, Small Heath
Birmingham B10 0UG, U.K.
Tel. 121-773-0137
Fax: 121-766-8577
e-mail: info@ipci-iv.co.uk
www.islamicvision.co.uk

IB Publisher Inc.
81 Bloomingdale Rd, Hicksville
NY 11801, USA
Tel. 516-933-1000
Fax: 516-933-1200
Toll Free: 1-888-560-3222
email: info@ibpublisher.com
www.ibpublisher.com

Printed in India

How to Use this Dictionary

Goodword Arabic Picture Dictionary for Kids is the perfect first reference book created to help your child learn Arabic in an easy and fun-filled way. Find out how you can get the most from your dictionary.

Words: Commonly used words that catch children's imagination.

Definitions: Easy-to-understand definitions put word-meaning and illustrations into context.

Illustrations: Colourful and amusing illustrations for quick understanding of each word.

Cc

Calender تَقْوِيمٌ
A **calendar** tells us day and date.
يُبَيِّنُ لَنَا التَّقْوِيمُ اليَوْمَ وَالتَّارِيخَ

Candle شَمْعَةٌ
The **candle** is burning out.
الشَّمْعَةُ تَحْتَرِقُ

Cafe مَقْهًى
The **café** is by the roadside.
المَقْهَى عَلَى جَانِبِ الطَّرِيقِ

Camel جَمَلٌ
The **camel** is the ship of the desert.
الجَمَلُ سَفِينَةُ الصَّحْرَاءِ

Candy حَلْوَى
The boy is licking a **candy**.
يَلْعَقُ الوَلَدُ حَلْوَى

Cake كِيكَةٌ
It's a cherry **cake**.
إِنَّهَا كِيكَةُ كَرَزٍ

Camera آلَةُ تَصْوِيرٍ
We take pictures with a **camera**.
نَلْتَقِطُ الصُّوَرَ بِآلَةِ تَصْوِيرٍ

Canoe كَانُوِي
A **canoe** is a kind of boat.
الكَانُوِي نَوْعٌ مِنَ القَوَارِبِ

Calculator آلَةٌ حَاسِبَةٌ
We can do maths on a **calculator**.
يُمْكِنُنَا أَدَاءُ الرِّيَاضِيَّاتِ عَلَى الآلَةِ الحَاسِبَةِ

Camp مُخَيَّمٌ
Camping in a forest can be fun.
قَدْ يَكُونُ التَّخْيِيمُ فِى الغَابَةِ مُمْتِعًا

Car سَيَّارَةٌ
He is proud to own a new **car**.
إِنَّهُ فَخُورٌ بِامْتِلَاكِ سَيَّارَةٍ جَدِيدَةٍ

10

Advertisement إِعْلَانٌ

A toothpaste **advertisement**.

إِعْلَانٌ عن مَعْجونِ أسْنَان

Alligator تِمسَاحٌ

Alligators live in water.

تعيشُ التَّمَاسيحُ في المَاءِ

Above فَوْق

Above the mountain, clouds.

فَوْقَ الجبلِ سُحُبٌ

Aeroplane طَائِرَةٌ

A happy **aeroplane**.

طَائِرَةٌ سعيدةٌ

Alphabet حُرُوفُ الهِجَاءِ

Some letters from the **alphabet**.

بَعْضُ حُرُوفِ الهِجَاء

Accident حَادِث

A car **accident**.

حَادِثُ سيَّارة

Afternoon بَعدَ الظُّهْر

An **afternoon** nap.

قيلُولَةُ بعدِ الظُّهْرِ

Ambulance سيَّارةُ إسْعَاف

An **ambulance** carries the sick.

سيَّارةُ إسْعَافٍ تَحْمِل المَرضَى

Actor مُمَثِّلٌ

The **actor** is singing.

الممثلُ يُغَنِّي

Alien مَخْلُوقٌ فَضَائِيٌّ

An **alien** from another planet.

مَخْلُوقٌ فَضَائيٌّ مِن كَوْكبٍ آخر

Animal حَيَوَانٌ

Lions and sheep are **animals**.

الأُسُودُ والخِرَافُ حَيَوَانَاتٌ

Ant نَمْلَة

The **ant** is singing.

النَّمْلَةُ تُغَنِّي

Aquarium حَوْضٌ

Fish can live in an **aquarium.**

يَسْتَطِيعُ السَّمكُ العَيْشَ في حَوضٍ

Astronaut رَائِدُ فَضَاء

An **astronaut** goes into space.

يَذهبُ رَائِدُ الفَضَاءِ إلى الفَضَاء

Antenna لاقِطُ إِشَارَة

Birds like to sit on **antennas.**

تُحِبُّ الطُّيورُ النُّزُولَ عَلى لاقِطِ الإشَارَة

Arrow سَهْم

An **arrow** gives us directions.

يَدُلُّنَا السَّهْمُ عَلى الاتِّجَاه

Astronomer فَلَكِيّ

An **astronomer** loves stars.

الفَلَكِيُّ يُحِبُّ النُّجُومَ

Apple تُفَّاحَةٌ

The **apple** has a worm in it.

في التفَّاحَةِ دُودَةٌ

Artist رَسَّام

An **artist** is painting.

رَسَّامٌ يَرْسُم

Atlas أطْلَس

An **atlas** has a lot of maps.

أطْلَسٌ يَحوِي خَرائِطَ كَثِيرة

Apron مِئْزَرٌ

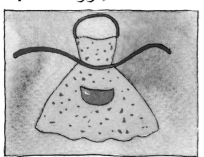

We wear an **apron** in the kitchen.

في المَطْبَخِ نَرتَدي مِئْزَرًا

Asleep نَائِمٌ

The boy is **asleep** in the class.

الصَّبِيُّ نائِمٌ في الصَّفِّ

Autumn الخَرِيف

Autumn comes before winter.

يَأتِي الخَرِيفُ قبلَ الشِّتَاء

Baker خَبَّازٌ

A **baker** with a cake.

خَبَّازٌ مَعَ كَعْكَةٍ

Banana مَوْزٌ

A monkey loves **bananas**.

القِرْدُ يُحِبُّ المَوْزَ

Baby رَضِيعٌ

A **baby** can cry really loud.

لَدَى الرَّضِيعِ المَقْدِرَةُ عَلَى الصُّرَاخِ عَالِيًا

Balcony شُرْفَةٌ

The king is standing on his **balcony**.

المَلِكُ واقِفٌ عَلَى شُرْفَتِه

Basket سَلَّةٌ

The **basket** is full of kittens.

السلّة مليئةٌ بِالقِطَطِ الصَّغِيرَةِ

Back ظَهْرٌ

Grandmother has a bad **back**.

ظَهْرُ الجَدَّةِ يُؤلِمُها

Ball كُرَةٌ

The boy is going to kick the **ball**.

سَيَرْكُلُ الوَلَدُ الكُرَةَ

Bathtub حَوْض اسْتِحْمَامٍ

A fat bear in a small **bathtub**.

دبٌّ سَمِينٌ فِي حَوْض اسْتِحْمَامٍ صَغِيرٍ

Bag حَقِيبَةٌ

This is my mother's **bag**.

هذهِ حقيبةُ أُمّي

Balloon بَالُونَةٌ

Balloons are going up in the sky.

بالوناتٌ تَرتَفِعُ فِي السَّمَاء

Battery بَطَّارِيَّةٌ

Batteries come in different sizes.

تَأتِي البَطَّارِياتُ فِي أحجامٍ مُخْتَلِفَةٍ

Beach شَاطِئٌ

A girl is playing on the **beach**.

بِنتٌ تَلْعَبُ عَلى الشَّاطِئِ

Behind خَلْفَ

The lion is **behind** the sheep.

الأَسَدُ خَلْفَ الخَرُوفِ

Bench مقْعَدٌ طويلٌ

A fat man is asleep on the **bench**.

رَجُلٌ سمينٌ نائِمٌ على مقْعَدٍ طَويلٍ

Bear دُبٌّ

The **bear** is a furry wild animal.

الدُّبُّ حَيَوانٌ فَرويٌّ مُتَوَحِّشٌ

Bell جَرَسٌ

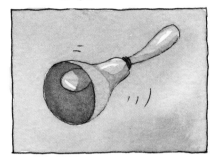

The **bell** rings "Ding dong".

يَدُقُّ الجَرَسُ "دينغ دونغ"

Between بَيْن

The fly is **between** two frogs.

الذُّبَابة بَيْنَ ضِفْدَعَيْن

Bed سَريرٌ

We love to sleep on a **bed**.

نَحْنُ نُحِبُّ النَّوْمَ على سَريرٍ

Below أَسْفَلَ

The sewer hole is **below** the man.

فَتْحَةُ المَجاري أَسْفَلَ الرُّجُلِ

Bicycle دَرَّاجَةٌ

A painting of a **bicycle**.

رَسْمٌ لِدَرَّاجَةٍ

Beehive خَلِيَّةُ نَحْلٍ

Bees live in a **beehive**.

يَعيشُ النَّحْلُ في خَلِيَّةٍ

Belt حِزَامٌ

This **belt** is so tight!

هَذَا الحِزامُ ضَيِّقٌ جِدًّا

Big كَبيرٌ

An elephant is a **big** animal.

الفيلُ حَيَوانٌ كَبيرٌ

Binoculars مِنْظَار مُقَرِّب

Binoculars make things look big.

يَجْعَلُ المِنْظَارُ المُقَرِّبُ الأَشْياءَ تَبْدو كَبيرَةً

Blackboard سَبُّورَةٌ

We write on the blackboard.

نَكْتُبُ عَلى السَّبُّورَةِ

Boat قَارِبٌ

An old man is rowing his boat.

شَيْخٌ يُجَدِّفُ قارِبَهُ

Bird طَائِرٌ

A bird is sitting on the branch.

طَائِرٌ نازِلٌ عَلى الفَرْعِ

Blanket بَطَّانِيَّةٌ

The blanket keeps us warm.

البَطَّانِيَّةُ تُدْفِئُنا

Book كِتَابٌ

A funny book is full of jokes.

كِتَابٌ مُسَلٍّ مَلِيءٌ بِالنِّكَاتِ

Birthday عِيدُ مِيلَادٍ

Here is a happy birthday cake.

هَاهُنا كَيْكَةُ عِيدِ مِيلَادٍ سَعِيدٍ

Blue أَزْرَقٌ

The blue alien looks sad.

المَخْلُوقُ الفَضَائِيُّ الأَزْرَقُ يَبْدو حَزِينًا

Bottle قَارُورَةٌ

There is a fish in the bottle.

سَمَكَةٌ فِي القَارُورَةِ

Biscuit بَسْكَوِيتٌ

We all love biscuits.

كُلُّنا نُحِبُّ البَسْكَوِيتَ

Board games أَلْعَابُ الطَّاوِلَةِ

We play board games at home.

نَلْعَبُ أَلْعَابَ الطَّاوِلَةِ فِي البَيْتِ

Box صُنْدُوقٌ

A cat is hiding under the box.

قِطَّةٌ مُخْتَبِئَةٌ تَحْتَ الصُّنْدُوقِ

Boy وَلَدٌ

The **boy** is smiling.

الوَلَدُ مُبْتَسِمٌ

Bridge جِسْرٌ

The **bridge** crosses the river.

يَمْتَدُّ الجِسْرُ فَوْقَ النَّهر

Bus حَافِلَةٌ

There goes a double-decker **bus**.

تلك حَافِلَةٌ ذات طَابِقَيْنِ

Branch فَرْعٌ

The **branch** has leaves on it.

على الفَرْعِ أُوْرَاقٌ

Bubble فُقَاعَةٌ

There are so many soap **bubbles**.

هناك كَثِيرٌ مِن فُقَاعَاتِ الصَّابُونِ

Butter زُبْدٌ

We love to eat bread with **butter**.

نُحِبُّ أَكْلَ الخُبْزِ بِالزُّبْدِ

Bread خُبْزٌ

Fresh **bread** smells good.

رَائِحَةُ الخُبْزِ الطَّازَجِ جَيِّدَةٌ

Bucket دَلْوٌ

A **bucket** is for cleaning.

الدَّلْوُ للتَّنْظِيفِ

Butterfly فَرَاشَةٌ

Butterflies have beautiful wings.

لِلفَرَاشَاتِ أَجْنِحَةٌ جَمِيلَةٌ

Breakfast فَطُورٌ

Breakfast is tasty with eggs.

الفَطُورُ لَذِيذٌ مَعَ البَيْضِ

Burrow جُحْرٌ

Rabbits live in **burrows**.

تَعِيشُ الأَرَانِبُ في الجُحُورِ

Button زِرٌّ

Buttons come in many shapes.

للأَزْرَارِ أَشْكَالٌ عِدَّةٌ

Calender تَقْوِيمٌ

A **calendar** tells us day and date.

يُبَيِّنُ لَنَا التَّقْوِيمُ اليَوْمَ وَالتَّارِيخَ

Candle شَمْعَةٌ

The **candle** is burning out.

الشَّمْعَةُ تَحْتَرِقُ

Cafe مَقْهًى

The **café** is by the roadside.

المَقْهَى على جَانِبِ الطَّرِيقِ

Camel جَمَلٌ

The **camel** is the ship of the desert.

الجَمَلُ سَفِينَةُ الصَّحْرَاءِ

Candy حَلْوَى

The boy is licking a **candy.**

يَلْعَقُ الولدُ حَلْوَى

Cake كِيكَةٌ

It's a cherry **cake.**

إنَّهَا كَيْكَةُ كَرَزٍ

Camera آلَةُ تَصْوِيرٍ

We take pictures with a **camera.**

نَلْتَقِطُ الصُّوَرَ بآلةِ تَصْوِيرٍ

Canoe كَأنُوِي

A **canoe** is a kind of boat.

الكَأنُوِي نَوْعٌ مِن القَوَارِبِ

Calculator آلَةٌ حَاسِبَةٌ

We can do maths on a **calculator.**

يُمْكِنُنَا أدَاءُ الرياضياتِ على الآلَةِ الحَاسِبَةِ

Camp مُخَيَّمٌ

Camping in a forest can be fun.

قد يكونُ التَّخْيِيمُ فِي الغَابَةِ مُمْتِعًا

Car سَيَّارَةٌ

He is proud to own a new **car.**

إنَّهُ فَخُورٌ بِامْتِلَاكِ سَيَّارَةٍ جديدَةٍ

Card بِطَاقَةٌ

This playing **card** is an ace.

بِطَاقَةُ اللَّعِبِ هَذِهِ آس

Caterpillar يُسْرُوعٌ

The hungry **caterpillar** eats leaves.

اليُسْرُوعُ الجَائِعُ يَأْكُلُ أوراقاً

Cereal حُبُوبٌ

We eat **cereal** with milk.

نَأْكُلُ الحُبوبَ مَعَ الحَلِيب

Carpet سَجَّادَةٌ

The cat flies on a magic **carpet.**

تَطِيرُ القِطَّةُ عَلَى سَجَّادَةٍ سِحْرِيَّةٍ

Cave كَهْفٌ

The bear lives in the **cave.**

يَعِيشُ الدُّبُّ فِي الكَهْفِ

Chair كُرْسِيٌّ

The cat sleeps on the rocking **chair.**

تَنَامُ القِطَةُ على الكُرْسِيِّ المُتَأَرْجِحِ

Carrot جَزَرٌ

The rabbit loves to eat a **carrot.**

يُحِبُّ الأَرْنَبُ أَكْلَ الجَزَر

Ceiling سَقْفٌ

The **ceiling** is a bit low.

السقفُ منخفضٌ قليلاً

Cheese جُبْنٌ

The mouse loves **cheese** very much.

يُحِبُّ الفَأْرُ الجُبْنَ كَثِيرًا

Cat قِطَّةٌ

Can you see a black **cat** at night?

هَلْ بِاسْتِطَاعَتِكَ رُؤْيَةُ قِطَّةٍ سَوْدَاءَ لَيْلاً؟

Cellphone هاتِفٌ مَحْمُولٌ

The **cellphone** is a small phone.

الهاتِفُ المَحْمُولُ صَغِيرُ الحَجْمِ

Chef طَاهِي

The **chef** is tossing a pizza.

يُقَلِّبُ الطَّاهِي بيتزا

Cherry جِيرِي

Mr. **Cherry** smiles at Mrs. **Cherry.**

يَبْتَسِمُ السَّيِّدُ جِيرِي فِي وَجْهِ السَّيِّدَةِ جِيرِي

Cinema سِينَما

Cinema halls have film shows.

تَعْرِضُ صَالاتُ السِّينَمَا العُرُوضَ السِّينمائِيَّة

Clothes مَلابِسُ

All winter **clothes** are warm.

جَمِيعُ المَلابِسِ الشِّتْوِيَّةِ دَافِئَةٌ

Chicken دَجَاجَةٌ

A giant **chicken** chases a man.

دَجَاجَةٌ عِمْلَاقَةٌ تُطَارِدُ رجلاً

City مَدِينَةٌ

A **city** has a lot of buildings.

مَدِينَةٌ كثيرةُ المَبَانِي

Cloud سَحَابَةٌ

The **clouds** are white and fluffy.

السُّحُبُ بَيْضاءُ ورَقِيقَةٌ

Chimney مِدْخَنَةٌ

A **chimney** is meant for smoke.

المِدخنةُ لإخراجِ الدُّخَانِ

Cliff جُرُف

The cat teeters on the **cliff** edge.

يتأرجَحُ القِطُ على حَافَّةِ الجُرُفِ

Clown مُهَرِّجٌ

The poor **clown** is sad.

المُهَرِّجُ المِسْكِينُ حَزِينٌ

Chocolate شُوكُولَاتَةٌ

A **chocolate** bar is delicious.

شُوكولَاتةٌ لَذِيذَةٌ

Clock ساعَةٌ

A **clock** tells us the time.

السَّاعَةُ تَدُلُّنَا عَلَى الوَقْتِ

Coat مِعطَفٌ

The fox is in a red **coat.**

الثَّعْلَبُ في مِعطفٍ أَحْمَر

Coconut جَوْزُ الهِنْدِ

Coconut trees grow by the sea.

تَنْمُو أَشْجَارُ جَوْزِ الهِنْدِ بِجَانِبِ البَحْرِ

Countryside رِيفٌ

The countryside is lovely.

الرِّيفُ جَمِيلٌ

Crow غُرَابٌ

The jolly crow is flying east.

الغُرَابُ المُبْتَهِجُ يَطِيرُ شَرْقاً

Comic قِصَّةٌ مُصَوَّرَةٌ

The boy is reading a comic.

يَقْرَأُ الولدُ قِصَّةً مُصَوَّرَةً

Cow بَقَرَةٌ

A cow gives us milk.

البَقَرة تُعْطِينَا اللَّبَنَ

Crowd حَشْدٌ

A crowd is a lot of people.

الحَشْدُ عَدَدٌ كَبِيرٌ مِن النَّاسِ

Computer حَاسُوبٌ

All computers have a mouse.

لِكُلِّ حَاسُوبٍ فَأْرَةٌ

Crane رَافِعَةٌ

A crane is a heavy machine.

الرَّافِعَةُ آلَةٌ ثَقِيلَةٌ

Cup كُوبٌ

A cup of morning tea is welcome.

مَرْحَبًا بِكُوبٍ مِن شاي الصَّباحِ

Cookies كَعْكٌ مُحَلًّى

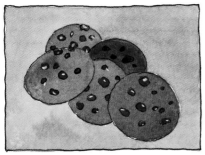

We love chocolate cookies too!

نحب كَعْكَ الشوكولاتِةِ المُحَلَّى كَذلِك!

Crayons ألوانٌ شَمْعِيَّةٌ

Crayons come in many colors.

تَأْتِي الأَلْوانُ الشَّمْعِيَّةُ في أَلْوانٍ عَدِيدَةٍ

Curtain سِتَارٌ

Kitty hides behind the curtain.

قِطَّةٌ صغيرةٌ تَخْتَبِئُ وَرَاءَ السِتَارِ

Day نَهَارٌ

The sun brightens the **day**.

الشَّمْسُ تُضِيءُ النَّهَارَ

Diagram رَسْمٌ بَيَانِيٌّ

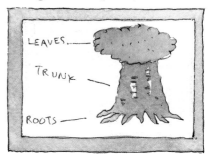

The **diagram** of a tree.

رُسُومٌ بيانيَّةٌ لِشَجَرةٍ

Daisy زَهْرَةُ الرَّبِيعِ

The **daisy** is a lovely white flower.

زَهْرَةُ الرَّبِيعِ زَهْرَةٌ جَمِيلَةٌ بَيْضَاءُ

Dentist دينتست

The **dentist** is a teeth doctor.

الدينتست هوطبيبُ الأسْنَانِ

Diamond مَاسٌ

The ring has a huge **diamond**.

على الخَاتَمِ مَاسَةٌ كبيرةٌ الحَجْمِ

Dam سَدٌّ

Dams are built across a river.

تُبْنَى السُّدودُ على الأنْهَارِ

Desert صَحْرَاءُ

It can be very hot in the **desert**.

يُمْكِن أن يَكونَ الطَّقْسُ حَارًّا جِدًّا في الصَّحْرَاءِ

Dice نَرْدٌ

Dots on **dice** mean numbers.

النِّقَاطُ عَلَى النَّرْدِ تَعْنِي أَرْقَامًا

Dark ظَلَامٌ

Who is hiding in the **dark**?

من مُخْتَبِئٌ في الظَّلامِ؟

Desk مَكْتَبٌ

He is sleeping at his **desk**.

هُوَ نَائِمٌ عَلَى مَكْتَبِهِ

Dictionary قَامُوسٌ

Here's a picture **dictionary**.

هذا قَامُوسٌ مُصَوَّرٌ

Different مُخْتَلِفٌ

They are very **different.**

هُم مُخْتَلِفُونَ جِدًّا

Doctor طَبِيبٌ/طَبِيبَةٌ

A **doctor** works in a hospital.

تَعْمَلُ الطَّبِيبَةُ فِي الْمُسْتَشْفَى

Dome قُبَّةٌ

Domes are round and big.

الْقِبَابُ مُسْتَدِيرَةٌ وَكَبِيرَةٌ

Dimple غَمَّازَةٌ

She has lovely **dimples.**

لَهَا غَمَّازَاتٌ جَمِيلَةٌ

Dog كَلْبٌ

Dogs don't like cats.

الْكِلَابُ لَا تُحِبُّ الْقِطَطَ

Door بَابٌ

The cat is knocking on the **door.**

يَطْرُقُ الْقِطُّ الْبَابَ

Dinosaur دِينَاصُور

A **dinosaur** is a huge animal.

الدِّينَاصُورُ حَيَوَانٌ ضَخْمٌ

Doll دُمْيَةٌ

A **doll** sits with a teddy bear.

دُمْيَةٌ موضوعَةٌ مَعَ لُعْبَةِ دُبٍّ

Dragon تِنِّينٌ

The **dragon** has very big wings.

لِلتِّنِّين أَجْنِحَةٌ كَبِيرَةٌ جِدًّا

Dirty وَسِخٌ

Babies get **dirty** easily.

يَتَّسِخُ الأَطْفالُ بِسُهُولَةٍ

Dolphin دُلْفِينٌ

The **dolphin** likes to jump a lot.

الدُّلْفين يُحِبُّ القَفْزَ كَثِيراً

Drawing رَسْمٌ

A **drawing** shows me and my cat.

الرَّسْمُ يُصَوِّرُنِي مَعَ قِطَّتِي

Dress لِبَاسٌ

It's a lovely white **dress.**

هذا لِبَاسٌ أَبْيَضُ جَمِيلٌ

Drink شَرَابٌ

We love a cool refreshing **drink.**

نُحِبُّ شَرَابًا بَارِدًا مُنْعِشاً

Drum طَبْلٌ

We bang a **drum** to make music.

نَدُقُّ الطَّبْلَ لِنَخْلُقَ مُوسِيقى

Duck بَطَّةٌ

Ducks can swim and walk too!

تَسْتَطِيعُ البَطَّةُ السِّبَاحَةَ والمَشْيَ كَذَلِكَ!

Earth الأَرْضُ

The **earth** is the planet we live on.

الأَرْضُ الكَوْكَبُ الَّذِي نَعِيشُ فِيهِ

East المَشْرِقُ

The sun rises in the **east.**

تَطْلُعُ الشّمسُ مِن المَشْرِقِ

Echo صَدًى

An **echo** is what comes back.

الصَّدَى رَجْعُ الصَّوْتِ

Edge حَافَّةٌ

The jug is just on the **edge.**

الإِبْرِيقُ عَلَى الحَافَّةِ تَمَامًا

Egg بَيْضَةٌ

This is a beautifully painted **egg.**

هذه بَيْضَةٌ مَرْسُومَةٌ فِي شَكْلٍ جَمِيلٍ

Elephant فِيلٌ

This **elephant** is so thin!

هَذَا الفِيلُ نَحِيلٌ جِدًّا!

Engine مُحَرِّكٌ

The cat is driving the **engine.**

يَقُودُ القِطُّ المحرِّكَ

Entrance مَدْخَلٌ

The tunnel has a huge **entrance.**

لِلنَّفَقِ مَدْخَلٌ عَظِيمٌ

Evening مَسَاءٌ

The **evening** sky is beautiful.

السَّمَاءُ جَمِيلَةٌ فِي المَسَاءِ

Envelope ظَرْفٌ

We post a letter in an **envelope.**

نَبْعَثُ الرِّسَالَةَ فِي ظَرْفٍ

Exhibition مَعْرَضٌ

Here's an **exhibition** of portraits.

هَذَا مَعْرَضٌ لِلصُّوَرِ الشَّخْصِيَّةِ

Face وَجْهٌ

A smiling **face** is always good.

الوَجْهُ المُبْتَسِمُ دَائِمًا حَسَنٌ

Environment بِيئَةٌ

Smoke pollutes the **environment.**

الدُّخَانُ يُلَوِّثُ البِيئَةَ

Exit مَخْرَجٌ

We leave by an **exit.**

نَخْرُجُ مِنَ المَخْرَجِ

Factory مَصْنَعٌ

The **factory** has many chimneys.

لِلمَصْنَعِ مَدَاخِنُ كَثِيرَةٌ

Escalator سُلَّمٌ كَهْرَبَائِيٌّ

An **escalator** is a moving stair.

السُّلَّمُ الكَهْرَبَائِيُّ هُوَ سُلَّمٌ نَاقِلٌ

Explorer مُسْتَكْشِفٌ

The **explorer** is fearless.

المُسْتَكْشِفُ مِقْدَامٌ

Fairy جِنِّيَّةٌ

A **fairy** is a magical girl.

الجِنِّيَّةُ فتاةٌ سحريَّةٌ

Fan مِرْوَحَةٌ

The **fan** makes us cool.

المِرْوَحَةُ تُنْعِشُنَا

Festival مَهْرَجَانٌ

We love to celebrate **festival**.

نحبُّ الاحتِفَالَ بالمَهْرَجَانَاتِ

Fireworks أَلْعَابٌ نَارِيةٌ

Fireworks are lit on festivals.

الأَلْعَابُ النَّارِيَّةُ تُطْلَقُ في المَهْرَجَانَاتِ

Farm مَزْرَعَةٌ

Farmers grow crops on a **farm**.

يُنَمِّي المُزَارِعُونَ مَحْصُولَاتِهِم في المَزْرَعَةِ

Finger أُصْبُعٌ

A bandaged **finger**.

أُصْبُعٌ مُضَمَّدٌ

First-aid الإِسْعَافَاتُ الأَوَّلِيَّةُ

The **First-aid** box is very useful.

صُنْدُوقُ الإِسْعَافَاتِ الأَوَّلِيَّةِ مُفِيدٌ جِدًّا

Feather رِيشَةٌ

This hat is made of **feathers**.

هَذِهِ القُبَّعَةُ مَصْنُوعَةٌ مِن الرِّيشِ

Fire نَارٌ

Fire is used for cooking too!

تُسْتَخْدَمُ النَّارُ للطَّبْخِ وَغَيْرِهِ!

Fish سَمَكٌ

There is always a bigger **fish**.

السَّمَكُ كبيرٌ وصغيرٌ

Fence سِيَاجٌ

The cat is dozing on a **fence**.

القِطَّةُ تَغْفُو عَلَى سِيَاجٍ

Fire truck سَيَّارَةُ إِطْفَاءٍ

The **fire truck** rushes to the fire.

سَيَّارَةُ الإِطْفَاءِ تنطلقُ مُسرعةً إلى النَّارِ

Flag عَلَمٌ

This **flag** is of the Cat Kingdom.

هَذا عَلَمُ مَمْلَكَةِ القِطَطِ

Flamingo طَائِرُ النُّحَامِ

Flamingos are large pink birds.

طُيُورُ النُّحَامِ كَبِيرَةُ الحَجْمِ وَرِدِيَّةُ اللَّوْنِ

Flowerpot أُصِيصٌ

A daisy **flowerpot** is pretty.

أُصِيصُ زَهْرَةِ الرَّبِيعِ جَمِيلٌ

Fountain نَافُورَةٌ

Fountains are beautiful.

النَّوَافِيرُ جَمِيلَةٌ

Flies ذُبَابٌ

Flies are small insects.

الذُّبَابُ حَشَرَاتٌ صَغِيرَةٌ

Fog ضَبَابٌ

It is very difficult to see in **fog**.

صَعْبٌ جِدًّا أَن نَرَى فِي الضَّبَابِ

Fox ثَعْلَبٌ

The **fox** is smartly dressed.

الثَّعْلَبُ مُرْتَدٍ مَلْبَسًا أَنِيقًا

Florist زَهَّارٌ

A **florist** sells flowers.

الزَّهَّارُ يَبِيعُ الزُّهُورَ

Footprint أَثَرُ قَدَمٍ

He discovered a giant **footprint**.

اكْتَشَفَ أَثَرَ قَدَمٍ عِمْلَاقَةٍ

Friend صَدِيقٌ

They are best **friends**.

هُمْ أَصْدِقَاءُ حَمِيمُونَ

Flower زَهْرَةٌ

Flowers come in many colours.

الزُّهُورُ مُتَعَدِّدَةُ الأَلْوَانِ

Fork شَوْكَةٌ

The **fork** is used to eat food.

تُسْتَخْدَمُ الشَّوْكَةُ لِتَنَاوُلِ الطَّعَامِ

Frog ضِفْدَعٌ

Frogs can jump very far.

تَسْتَطِيعُ الضَّفَادِعُ القَفْزَ مَسَافَةً طَوِيلَةً جِدًّا

Frost صَقِيعٌ

It is very cold on a **frosty** day.

يَوْمٌ صَقِيعٌ شَدِيدُ البَرْدِ

Gg

Giant عِمْلَاقٌ

Hello!

The fairy tale **giant** is huge.

عِمْلَاقُ حِكَايَاتِ الجِنّ ضَخْمٌ

Fruit فَاكِهَةٌ

Monkeys love all kind of **fruits.**

القُرُودُ تُحِبُّ كُلَّ أَنْوَاعِ الفَاكِهَةِ

Garage مِرْآبٌ

The car is in the **garage**.

السَّيَّارَةُ فِي المِرْآبِ

Giraffe زَرَافَةٌ

Giraffes are very tall.

الزَّرَافَاتُ طَوِيلَةٌ جِدًّا

Fur فَرْوٌ

A **fur** coat keeps us warm.

مِعْطَفُ الفَرْوِ يُدْفِئُنَا

Garden حَدِيقَةٌ

The boy relaxes in the **garden.**

الوَلَدُ يَرْتَاحُ فِي الحَدِيقَةِ

Girl بِنْتٌ

Girls wear ribbons in their hair.

تَرْتَدِي البَنَاتُ أَشْرِطَةً فِي شُعُورِهِنَّ

Furniture أَثَاثٌ

Every house needs **furniture.**

كُلُّ بَيْتٍ يَحْتَاجُ أَثَاثًا

Gate بَوَّابَةٌ

CATS NOT ALLOWED

MR. MOUSE

A tall **gate** keeps out cats.

البَوَّابَةُ العَالِيَةُ حَاجِزَةٌ لِلقِطَطِ

Glass زُجَاجٌ

The cleaner is wiping the **glass.**

المُنَظِّفُ يَمْسَحُ الزُّجَاجَ

Globe كُرَةٌ جُغْرَافِيَةٌ

A **globe** is a ball showing countries.

الكُرَةُ الجُغْرَافِيَّةُ تُظْهِرُ الأَقْطَارَ

Grass عُشْبٌ

The girl is lying in the **grass.**

البِنتُ مُسْتَلْقِيَةٌ عَلَى العُشْبِ

Gloves قُفَازَاتٍ

The cat wears red boxing **gloves.**

يَرْتَدِي القِطُّ قُفَازَاتٍ مُلَاكَمَةٍ حَمْرَاءَ

Green أَخْضَرُ / خَضْرَاءُ

She just loves **green** colour.

هِيَ تُحِبُّ اللَّوْنَ الأَخْضَرَ فَقَطْ

Hair شَعَرٌ

This girl has very long **hair.**

شَعَرُ البِنتِ طَوِيلٌ جِدًّا

Goat مَاعِزٌ

This **goat** has got pointed horns.

هَذَا المَاعِزُ قُرُونُهُ حَادَّةٌ

Greenhouse بَيْتٌ زُجَاجِيٌّ

Some plants grow in **greenhouses.**

بَعْضُ النَّبَاتَاتِ تَنْمُو فِي بُيُوتٍ زُجَاجِيَّةٍ

Half نِصْفٌ

He has eaten **half** of the cake.

قَدْ أَكَلَ نِصْفَ الكَيْكَةِ

Grapes عِنَبٌ

Grapes can be green or black.

قَدْ يَكُونُ العِنَبُ أَخْضَرَ أَوْ أَسْوَدَ

Gymnastics جُمْبَازٌ

The boy does **gymnastics.**

يُمَارِسُ الوَلَدُ رِيَاضَةَ الجُمْبَازِ

Hand يَدٌ

A **hand** has five fingers.

لِليَدِ خَمْسَةُ أَصَابِع

21

Handkerchief مَنْدِيلٌ

He sneezes into his **handkerchief.**

يَعْطِسُ فِي مَنْدِيلِهِ

Happy سَعِيدٌ

A **happy** cat.

قِطٌّ سَعِيدٌ

Harbor مَرْسَى

The dog strolls along the **harbor.**

الكَلْبُ هَائِمٌ فِي المَرْسَى

Harmonica هَارْمُونِيكَا

A **harmonica** is played by mouth.

تُؤَدَّى الهَارْمُونِيكَا بِالفَمِ

Hat قُبَّعَةٌ

The boy is wearing his father's **hat.**

الوَلَدُ مُرْتَدٍ قُبَّعَةَ أَبِيهِ

Hay قَشٌّ

The cat is sleeping in **hay.**

القِطُّ نَائِمٌ عَلَى القَشِّ

Heavy ثَقِيلٌ

The baby elephant is too **heavy.**

الفِيلُ الصَّغِيرُ وَزْنُهُ ثَقِيلٌ جِدًّا

Hedge حَافَّةٌ

The thief is hiding behind the **hedge.**

اللِّصُّ مُخْتَبِئٌ خَلْفَ الحَاجِزِ الشَّجَرِيِّ

Helicopter مِرْوَحِيَّةٍ

Helicopter rotors are like a fan.

أَرْيَاشُ المِرْوَحِيَّةِ تُشْبِهُ المِرْوَحَةَ

Helmet خَوْذَةٌ

The kids are wearing **helmets.**

الصِّغَارُ يرتَدُونَ خَوْذَاتٍ

High عَالِي

The cat lives in a **high** building.

القِطُّ يَعِيشُ فِي مَبْنًى عَالٍ

Hill تَلٌّ

The road leads to the **hill.**

الطَّرِيقُ تُؤَدِّي إِلَى التَّلِّ

Hippopotamus   فَرَسُ بَحْرٍ

The **Hippopotamus** floats in water.

فَرَسُ بَحْرٍ طَافٍ عَلَى المَاءِ

III   مَرِيض/ مَرِيضة

The girl stays in bed! She's **ill**.

البِنْتُ تَبْقَى عَلَى السَّرِير! إِنَّها مَرِيضَةٌ

Horse   جَوَادٌ

The cat jumps on a rocking **horse**.

يَقْفِزُ القِطُّ عَلَى جَوَادٍ مُتَأَرْجِح

Iceberg   كُتْلَةٌ جَلِيدِيَّةٌ

The penguin stands on the **iceberg**.

يَقِفُ البِطرِيقُ عَلَى كُتْلَةٍ جَلِيدِيَّةٍ

Injury   إِصَابَةٌ

Injury hurts a lot!

تُؤْلِمُ الإِصَابَةُ كَثِيرًا

Hospital   مُسْتَشْفَى

This **hospital** is for sick cats.

هَذَا المُسْتَشْفَى لِلقِطَطِ المَرِيضَةِ

Ice-cream   كِرِيمٌ مُثَلَّجٌ

He loves big scoops of **ice-cream**.

يُحِبُّ قِطَعَ الكِرِيمِ المُثَلَّجِ الكَبِيرَةِ

Ink   حِبْرٌ

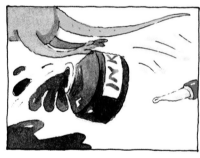

The mouse spills the **ink**.

يُرِيقُ الفَأْرُ الحِبرَ

Hot-air balloon   مِنطَادٌ

This is a **hot-air balloon**.

هَذَا مِنطَادٌ

Icicle   مُدَبَّبَةُ ثَلْجٍ

Icicles are formed when it snows.

تَتَشَكَّلُ مُدَبَّبَاتُ الثَّلْجِ عِندَ تَسَاقُطِ الجَلِيدِ

Insects   حَشَرَاتٌ

There are many kinds of **insects**.

لِلحَشَرَاتِ أَنواعٌ كَثِيرَةٌ

Instrument آلَةٌ

A group of musical **instruments**.

مَجْمُوعَةُ آلَاتٍ مُوسِيقِيَّةٍ

Jeans بِنْطَالُ جِينزٍ

A pair of **jeans** on the grass.

بِنْطَالُ جِينزٍ عَلَى العُشْبِ

Invitation دَعْوَةٌ

An **invitation** to a birthday party.

دَعْوَةُ حَفْلِ عِيدِ مِيلَادٍ

Jacket مِعْطَفٌ خَفِيفٌ

The cat wears a green **jacket**.

يَلْبَسُ القِطُّ مِعْطَفًا خَفِيفًا أَخْضَرَ

Jellyfish قِنْدِيلُ البَحْرِ

Jellyfish swim in the sea.

يَسْبَحُ قِنْدِيلُ البَحْرِ فِي البَحْرِ

Iron مِكْوَاةٌ

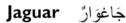

A very hot **iron** spoils your dress.

تُفْسِدُ المِكْوَاةُ شَدِيدَةُ الحَرَارَةِ مَلْبَسَكَ

Jaguar جَاغَوَارٌ

A jolly **jaguar**.

جَاغوارٌ مُبْتَهِجٌ

Jewel جَوْهَرَةٌ

The lady is laden with **jewels**.

السَّيِّدَةُ تَرْتَدِي كَثِيرًا بِالجَوَاهِرِ

Island جَزِيرَةٌ

A small **island** in a big sea.

جَزِيرَةٌ صَغِيرَةٌ فِي بَحْرٍ كَبِيرٍ

Jam مُرَبَّى

The cat loves strawberry **jam**.

يُحِبُّ القِطُّ مُرَبَّى الفَرَاوْلَةِ

Jigsaw لُعْبَةُ بَازِلٍ

This is a tough **jigsaw** puzzle.

لُعْبَةُ البَازِلِ هَذِهِ صَعْبَةٌ

Jug إِبْرِيقٌ

The **jug** is full of orange juice.

الإِبْرِيقُ مَلِيءٌ بِعَصِيرِ البُرْتُقَالِ

Juggler رَامِي الكُرَاتِ

A **juggler** knows many tricks.

يَعْرِفُ رَامِي الكُرَاتِ حِيَلاً كَثِيرَةً

Juice عَصِيرٌ

Juice is made from oranges.

هَذَا عَصِيرُ البُرْتُقَالِ

Jump قَفْزٌ

The cow **jumped** over the moon.

قَفَزَتِ البَقَرَةُ فَوْقَ الهِلَالِ

Kaleidoscope مِشْكَالٌ

A beautiful **kaleidoscope.**

مِشْكَالٌ جَمِيلٌ

Kangaroo كَنْغَرٌ

A **kangaroo** can leap really high.

يستطيعُ الكَنْغَرُ القَفْزَ عَالِياً حقًّا

Kettle غَلَّايَةٌ

The **kettle** is steaming.

الغَلَّايَةُ تَنْفُثُ بُخَاراً

Key مِفْتَاحٌ

A bunch of **keys** on a keychain.

مَجْمُوعَةُ مَفَاتِيحٍ عَلَى سِلْسِلَةِ مَفَاتِيحٍ

King مَلِكٌ

The **king** of the Cat Kingdom.

مَلِكُ مَمْلَكَةِ القِطَطِ

Kingfisher رَفْرَافٌ

Kingfishers like seafood.

تُحِبُّ الرَّفَارِفُ طَعَامَ البَحْرِ

Kitchen مَطْبَخٌ

The cat is in her **kitchen.**

القِطَّةُ فِي مَطْبَخِهَا

Kite طَائِرَةٌ وَرَقِيَّةٌ

It is too windy to fly a **kite**.

يَتَعَذَّرُ إِرْسَالُ طَائِرَةٍ وَرَقِيَّةٍ لِشِدَّةِ الرِّيَاحِ

Ll

Ladybird دُعْسُوقَةٌ

A **ladybird** is a tiny insect.

الدُّعْسُوقَةُ حَشَرَةٌ صَغِيرَةٌ

Knapsack حَقِيبَةُ ظَهْرٍ

The boy is carrying a heavy **knapsack**.

يَحْمِلُ الوَلَدُ حَقِيبَةَ ظَهْرٍ ثَقِيلَةً

Label عَلَامَةُ سِعْرٍ

The girl is looking at the **label**.

تَنْظُرُ البِنْتُ إِلَى عَلَامَةِ السِّعْرِ

Lake بُحَيْرَةٌ

The cat is resting at a quiet **lake**.

القِطَّةُ تَسْتَرِيحُ عِندَ بُحَيْرَةٍ هَادِئَةٍ

Knot عُقْدَةٌ

The silly snake tied itself in a **knot**.

رَبَطَ الثُّعْبَانُ السَّخِيفُ نَفْسَهُ فِي شَكْلِ عُقْدَةٍ

Lace رِبَاطٌ

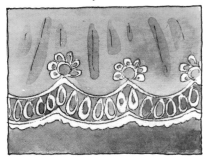

A table cover with white **lace**.

غِطَاءُ طَاوِلَةٍ بِرِبَاطٍ أَبْيَض

Lamp مِصْبَاحٌ

The boy sleeps under a table **lamp**.

يَنَامُ الوَلَدُ تَحْتَ مِصْبَاحِ طَاوِلَةٍ

Koala كُوَالَا

Koalas like to cling to trees.

يُحِبُّ الكُوَالَا التَّعَلُّقَ بِالأَشْجَارِ

Ladder سُلَّم

The cat is climbing a **ladder**.

القِطُّ يَتَسَلَّقُ سُلَّمًا

Laptop حَاسُوبٌ مَحْمُولٌ

A monkey is typing on his **laptop**.

القِرْدُ يَكْتُبُ عَلَى حَاسُوبِهِ المَحْمُولِ

Lawnmower جَزَّازَةُ عُشْبٍ

Lawnmower cuts grass.

جَزَّازَةُ العُشْبِ تَقُصُّ العُشْبَ

Leaf وَرَقَةُ شَجَرٍ

Someone is hiding in the **leaves.**

شَخْصٌ مُخْتَبِئٍ خَلْفَ وَرَقِ الشَّجَرِ

Leg رِجْلٌ

We have two **legs**; animals have four.

لَدَيْنَا رِجْلَانِ ولَدَى الحَيَوَانَاتِ أَرْبَعٌ

Lemon لَيْمُونٌ

The **lemon** has a tangy taste.

لِلْيَمُونِ نَكْهَةٌ قَوِيَّةٌ

Letter رِسَالَةٌ

The small girl is posting a **letter.**

البِنتُ الصَّغِيرَةُ تَبْعَثُ رِسَالةً

Library مَكْتَبَةٌ

A **library** has all kinds of books.

تَحْوِي المَكْتَبَةُ كُلَّ أَنْوَاعِ الكُتُبِ

Life jacket سُتْرَةُ نَجَاةٍ

Life jackets are for our safety.

سُتْرَاتُ النَّجَاةِ لِسَلَامَتِنَا

Light خَفِيفٌ

See! It is so **light** for me.

أُنْظُرْ! إِنَّهُ خَفِيفٌ جِدًّا بِالنِّسْبَةِ لِي

Lighthouse مَنَارَةٌ

Lighthouses show ships the rocks.

تُظْهِرُ المَنَارَاتُ الصُّخُورَ لِلسُّفُنِ

Lightning بَرْقٌ

Lightning can be dangerous.

قَدْ يَكُونُ البَرْقُ خَطِرًا

Lion أَسَدٌ

The **lion** is the king of the jungle.

الأَسَدُ مَلِكُ الغَابَةِ

Lock قُفْلٌ

The **lock** on the door is so big!

قُفْلُ البَابِ كَبِيرٌ جِدًّا!

Mm

Magnet مَغْنَاطِيسٌ

The **magnet** attracts the nail.

يَجْذِبُ المَغْنَاطِيسُ المِسْمَارَ

Menu قَائِمَةُ طَعَامٍ

A **menu** lists a cafe's dishes.

تَسْرُدُ القَائِمَةُ أَطْبَاقَ مَقْهى

Machine آلَةٌ

The scientist with his **machine.**

العَالِمُ مَعَ آلَتِهِ

Map خَرِيطَةٌ

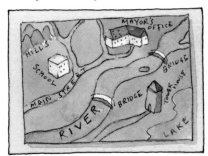

The **map** tells us about places.

تُخْبِرُنا الخَرِيطَةُ عَنِ الأَمَاكِنِ

Microwave ميكروويف

Microwaves cook food quickly.

تُعِدُّ الميكروويفاتُ الطَّعَامَ سَرِيعًا

Magazine مَجَلَّةٌ

The girl is reading a **magazine.**

تَقْرَأُ الفَتَاةُ مَجَلَّةً

Mask قِنَاعٌ

The boy is wearing a **mask.**

يَرتَدِي الوَلَدُ قِنَاعًا

Milk لَبَنٌ

The cow gives us **milk.**

تُعْطِينَا البَقَرَةُ لَبَنًا

Magic سِحْرِيٌّ / سِحْرِيَّة

The performer does **magic** tricks.

الحَاوِي يُؤَدِّي خِدَعًا سِحْرِيَةً

Medicine دَوَاءٌ

We take **medicine** when ill.

نَتَنَاوَلُ الدَّوَاءَ عِندَ المَرَض

Mirror مِرْآةٌ

The cat sees itself in the **mirror.**

تَنْظُرُ القِطَّةُ إلى نَفْسِها في المِرْآةِ

Money مَالٌ

My rich uncle is rolling in **money**.

عمي الغني يسبحُ في المَالِ

Motorcycle دَرَّاجة بُخَارِيَّةٌ

A cat on a **motorcycle**.

قِطَّةٌ عَلَى دَرَّاجَة بُخَارِيَّةٍ

Mud وَحْلٌ

The naughty girl plays in **mud**.

تَلْعَبُ البِنتُ المُزْعِجَةُ فِي الوَحْلِ

Monkey قِرْدٌ

A wise **monkey**.

قِرْدٌ حَكِيمٌ

Mountain جَبَلٌ

A cat on a **mountain** top.

قِطَّةٌ عَلَى قِمَّةِ جَبَلٍ

Muffin كَيْكُ الفَاكِهَةِ الصَّغِيرُ

He likes **muffins** very much.

هو يُحِبُّ كَيْكَ الفَاكِهَةِ الصَّغِيرَ جِدًّا

Moon قَمَرٌ

Dogs often howl on a full **moon**.

كَثِيراً مَّا تَعْوِي الكِلَابُ عِند اكتِمَال القَمَر

Mouse فَأْرٌ

The **mouse** lives in a hole.

يَعِيشُ الفَأْرُ في جُحْرٍ

Museum مُتْحَفٌ

A cat in the Cat **Museum**.

قِطَّةٌ فِي مُتْحَفِ القِطَطِ

Morning صَبَاحٌ

Wake up, it's a lovely **morning**.

اسْتَيْقِظْ، إنَّهُ صَبَاحٌ جَمِيلٌ

Moustache شَارِبٌ

Men grow many kinds of **moustache**.

يُنَمِّي الرِّجَالُ أنْوَاعًا عَدِيدَةً مِن الشَّوَارِبِ

Mushroom مَشْرُومٌ

The dwarf sits on a **mushroom**.

يَجْلِسُ القَزَمُ عَلَى المَشْرُوم

Necklace عِقْدٌ

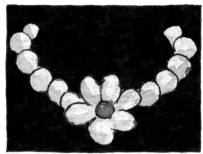

A pretty pearl **necklace**.

عِقْدٌ جَمِيلٌ مِنَ اللُّؤْلُؤِ

Net شَبَكَةٌ

The cat chases the mouse with a **net**.

تُطَارِدُ القِطَّةُ الفَأْرَ وَمَعَهَا شَبَكَةٌ

Nail مِسْمَارٌ

The **nail** doesn't like the hammer.

المِسْمَارُ لا يُحِبُّ المِطْرَقَةَ

Needle إِبْرَةٌ

Don't use a **needle** to prick.

لا تَسْتَخْدِمْ إِبْرَةً لِلْوَخْزِ

Newspaper صَحِيفَةٌ

The cat is reading a **newspaper**.

تَقْرَأُ القِطَّةُ صَحِيفَةً

Name اسْمٌ

What is your name?

*#%o#?

We all have got some **name**.

لِكُلٍّ مِنَّا اسْمٌ مَّا

Neighbour جَارٌ

Neighbours like to chat.

يُحِبُّ الجِيرَانُ الدَّرْدَشَةَ

Night لَيْلٌ

Everyone sleeps at **night**.

كُلُّ النَّاسِ يَنَامُونَ بِاللَّيْلِ

Nature طَبِيعَةٌ

A beautiful view of **nature**.

مَنْظَرٌ جَمِيلٌ مِنَ الطَّبِيعَةِ

Nest عُشٌّ

The baby bird is sitting in the **nest**.

الطَّائِرُ الصَّغِيرُ قَابِعٌ فِي العُشِّ

North شِمَالٌ

The bird is flying **north**.

الطَّائِرُ مُتَّجِهٌ نَحْوَ الشِّمَالِ

Notebook مُذَكِّرَةٌ

A **notebook** with a pencil.

مُذَكِّرَةٌ وَقَلَمُ رَصَاصٍ

Numbers أَرْقَامٌ

The alien tries to read **numbers**.

يُحَاوِلُ المَخْلُوقُ الفَضَائِيُّ قِرَاءَةَ الأَرْقَامِ

Nurse مُمَرِّضَةٌ

The **nurse** comes with an injection.

تَأْتِي المُمَرِّضَةُ وَمَعَهَا حُقْنَةٌ

Nuts جَوْزٌ

Squirrels like to collect **nuts**.

تُحِبُّ السَّنَاجِبُ جَمْعَ الجَوْزِ

Ocean مُحِيطٌ

The world has five **oceans**.

فِي العَالَمِ خَمْسَةُ مُحِيطَاتٍ

Octopus أُخْطُبُوطٌ

The **octopus** has eight legs.

لِلْأُخْطُبُوطِ ثَمَانِيَةُ أَرْجُلٍ

Office مَكْتَبٌ

My father works in an **office**.

يَعْمَلُ أَبِي فِي مَكْتَبٍ

Old مُسِنٌّ

An **old** man is dancing.

رجلٌ مُسِنٌّ يَرْقُصُ

Optician نَظَّارَاتِيٌّ

An **optician** is an eye doctor.

النَّظَّارَاتِيُّ هُوَ صَانِعُ عدَسَاتِ النَّظَرِ

Orange بُرْتُقَالٌ

A jug full of **orange** juice.

إِبْرِيقٌ مَلِيءٌ بِعَصِيرِ البُرْتُقَالِ

Orchard بُسْتَانٌ

An **orchard** has a lot of fruit trees.

فِي البُسْتَانِ كَثِيرٌ مِن أَشْجَارِ الفَاكِهَةِ

Ostrich نَعَامَةٌ

The angry **ostrich** is after the cat.

النَّعَامَةُ الغَاضِبَةُ تُطارِدُ القِطَّةَ

Parachute مِظَلَّةٌ

A rough **parachute** landing.

هُبوطٌ مِظَلِّيُّ قَاسٍ

Outline مُخَطَّطٌ

An **outline** of an elephant.

مُخَطَّطٌ لِفِيلٍ

Paint دِهَانٌ

Yellow, green and red **paint.**

دِهَانٌ أَصْفَرُ، وَأَخْضَرُ وَأَحْمَرُ

Parcel طَرْدٌ

The girl received a big **parcel.**

تَسَلَّمَتِ البِنْتُ طَرْدًا كَبيراً

Oven فُرْنٌ

Ovens are used to bake cakes.

تُسْتَخْدَمُ الأَفْرانُ لِخَبْزِ الكَيْكِ

Panda بَانْدَا

The cuddly baby **panda.**

البَانْدَا الصَّغيرُ المَحْبوبُ

Park مُنْتَزَهٌ

All cities have **parks.**

كُلُّ المُدُنِ فيها مُنْتَزَهاتٌ

Owl بُومَةٌ

The **owl** stays awake at night.

تَظَلُّ البُومَةُ مُسْتَيْقِظَةً طوالَ اللَيْلِ

Paper وَرَقٌ

A poster is printed on **paper.**

مُلْصَقٌ مَطْبوعٌ عَلَى وَرَقٍ

Parrot بَبْغَاءُ

Parrots can learn to talk.

تَسْتَطيعُ طُيورُ البَبْغَاءِ تَعَلُّمَ الكَلامِ

Pasta مَكَرونَةٌ

The girl is eating **pasta**.

تَأْكُلُ البِنتُ مَكَرونةً

Path طَرِيقٌ

This **path** leads into the forest.

تُؤَدّي هَذِهِ الطَّرِيقُ إِلَى الغَابَةِ

Pearl لُؤْلُؤٌ

Pearls are found in the sea.

تُوجَدُ اللَّآلِئُ فِي البَحْرِ

Peas بَازِلَّاءُ

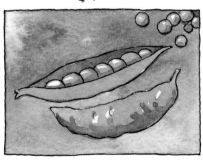

Pea is used as vegetable.

يُسْتَخْدَمُ البَازِلَّاءُ مثل الخضر

Pelican بَجَعٌ

Pelicans love to eat fish.

يُحِبُّ البَجَعُ أَكْلَ السَّمَكِ

Penguin بِطْرِيقٌ

A **penguin** with glasses.

بِطْرِيقٌ يَضَعُ نَظَّارَاتٍ

Photographs صُوَرٌ

Family **photographs**.

صُوَرٌ عَائِلِيَّةٌ

Piano بِيَانُو

The musician is playing a **piano**.

يَعْزِفُ المُوسِيقَارُ عَلَى البِيَانُو

Picnic نُزْهَةٌ

Picnics are fun!

النُزهَاتُ مُمْتِعَةٌ

Picture صُورَةٌ

A **picture** of the king of jungle.

صُورَةٌ لِمَلِكِ الغَابَةِ

Piece قِطْعَةٌ

A **piece** of yummy cake.

قِطْعَةُ كَيْكٍ لَذِيذٍ

Pigeon حَمَامَةٌ

The **pigeon** is listening to music.

تَسْتَمِعُ الحَمَامَةُ إِلَى المُوسِيقَى

Pillar عَمُودٌ

A **crow** is perched on a pillar.

غُرَابٌ نازِلٌ عَلَى عَمُودٍ

Pizza بِيتْزَا

The **pizza** has a lot of cheese.

البِيتْزَا فِيهَا جُبْنٌ كَثِيرٌ

Playground مَلْعَبٌ

We play in a **playground**.

نَلْعَبُ فِي مَلْعَبٍ

Pillow وِسَادَةٌ

The cat is napping on a **pillow**.

القِطَّةُ فِي سِنَةٍ عَلى وِسَادَةٍ

Planet كَوْكَبٌ

The Universe has many **planets**.

فِي الكَوْنِ عَدِيدٌ مِن الكَوَاكِبِ

Pocket جَيْبٌ

The fox wears a green coat with **pockets**.

يَرْتَدِي الثَّعْلَبُ مِعْطَفًا أَخْضَرَ بِهِ جُيُوبٌ

Pineapple أَنَانَاسٌ

A couple of friendly **pineapples**.

زَوْجٌ مِن أَنَانَاسٍ مُحَبَّبٍ

Plant كَوْكَبٌ

Some potted **plants**.

بَعْضُ النَّبَاتِ فِي أَصِيصٍ

Police officer ضَابِطُ شُرْطَةٍ

A tough **police officer**.

ضَابِطُ شُرْطَةٍ حَازِمٌ

Pink وَرْدِيٌّ

Pamela likes everything in **pink**.

تُحِبُّ بَامِيلا كُلَّ شَيْءٍ وَرْدِيَّ اللَّوْنِ

Platform رَصِيفٌ

A railway **platform**.

رَصِيفُ سِكَّةِ حَدِيدٍ

Pomegranate رُمَّانٌ

The **pomegranate** is a juicy fruit.

الرُّمَّانُ فَاكِهَةٌ غَنِيَّةٌ بالعَصِيرِ

Postcard   بِطَاقَةٌ بَرِيدِيَّةٌ

An invitation on a **postcard**.

دَعْوَةٌ عَلَى بِطَاقَةٍ بَرِيدِيَّةٍ

Queue   طَابُورٌ

We line up in a **queue**.

نَصْطَفُّ في طَابُورٍ

Prize   جَائِزَةٌ

The elephant won the first **prize**.

فَازَ الفِيلُ بِالجَائِزَةِ الأُولَى

Quarter   رُبْعٌ

A cake divided into **quarters**.

كَيْكَةٌ مَقْسُومَةٌ عَلَى أَرْبَاعٍ

Quiet   هَادِئٌ

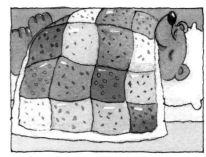

Please be **quiet**!

يُرْجَى الهُدُوءُ

Puppet   دُمْيَةٌ

The cat is playing with its **puppet**.

تَلْعَبُ القِطَّةُ بِدُمْيَتِهَا

Queen   مَلِكَةٌ

The **queen** is sitting on her throne.

المَلِكَةُ جَالِسَة عَلَى عَرْشِهَا

Quilt   لِحَافٌ

The bear is sleeping under a **quilt**.

الدُّبُّ نَائِمٌ تَحْتَ لِحَافٍ

Purse   حَقِيبَةُ يَدٍ

The cat with her new red **purse**.

القِطَّةُ تَحْمِلُ حَقِيبَةَ يَدِهَا الحَمْرَاءَ الجَدِيدَةَ

Question   سُؤَالٌ

'What is a question?' is a **question**.

"ما مَعْنَى سُؤَالٌ"؟ مَعْنَاهُ سؤالٌ!

Quiz   مُسَابَقَةٌ

A **quiz** show on Jungle TV.

مُسَابَقَةٌ عَلَى تِلِفِزْيُون قَنَاةِ جُنْغِل

Rr

Rain مَطَرٌ

Children enjoy the **rain**.

يَسْتَمْتِعُ الأَطْفَالُ بِالمَطَرِ

Refrigerator ثَلَّاجَةٌ

Uh oh, the **refrigerator** is empty!

أوه.. آه، الثَّلَّاجَةُ فَارِغَةٌ!

Rabbit أَرْنَبٌ

Rabbits cannot resist carrots.

لا تَسْتَطِيعُ الأَرَانِبُ مُقَاوَمَةَ الجَزَرِ

Rainbow قَوْسُ قُزَحٍ

The **rainbow** has seven colours.

قَوْسُ القُزَحِ لَهُ سَبْعَةُ أَلْوَانٍ

Restaurant مَطْعَمٌ

The cat dines in a **restaurant**.

يَتَنَاوَلُ القِطُّ العَشَاءَ فِي مَطْعَمٍ

Race سِبَاقٌ

The monkeys are having a sack **race**.

تَلْعَبُ القُرُودُ لُعْبَةَ سِبَاقِ الكِيسِ

Red أَحْمَر

The **red** alien has four eyes.

المَخْلُوقُ الفَضَائِيُّ الأَحْمَرُ لَهُ أَرْبَعَةُ عُيُونٍ

Rhinoceros وَحِيدُ قَرْنٍ

The **rhinoceros** chases the cat.

يُطَارِدُ وَحِيدُ القَرْنِ القِطَّةَ

Radio رَادِيُو

The bear is listening to the **radio**.

يَسْتَمِعُ الدُّبُّ إِلَى الرَّادِيُو

Reflection انعِكَاسٌ

The mirror shows our **reflection**.

تُظْهِرُ المِرآةُ انعِكَاسَنَا

Ribbon شَرِيطٌ

The girl is wearing a lovely **ribbon**.

البِنْتُ مُرتديةٌ شَرِيطًا جَميلاً

Ring حَلْقَةٌ

A **ring** of fire.

حَلْقَةٌ مِن نَارٍ

Rock صَخْرَةٌ

The frog is resting on the **rock.**

يَسْتَرِيحُ الضِّفْدَعُ عَلَى الصَّخْرَةِ

Rope حَبْلٌ

The cat skips with a **rope.**

تَقْفِزُ القِطَّةُ بِحَبْلٍ

River نَهْرٌ

A **river** passing through the desert.

نَهْرٌ يَقْطَعُ الصَّحْرَاءَ

Rocket صَارُوخٌ

The **rocket** takes us into space.

يَأْخُذُنَا الصَّارُوخُ إِلَى الفَضَاءِ

Rose وَرْدَةٌ

The Sultan is fond of **roses.**

السُّلْطَانُ مُولَعٌ بِالْوُرُودِ

Road طَرِيقٌ

The **road** that leads to the city.

الطَّرِيقُ المُؤَدِّيَةُ إِلَى المَدِينَةِ

Roof سَقْفٌ

A black cat on a red **roof.**

قِطَّةٌ سَوْدَاءُ عَلَى سَقْفٍ أَحْمَرَ

Roundabout دَوَّارٌ

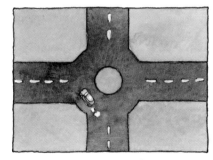

The car at a **roundabout.**

السَّيَّارَةُ عِندَ دَوَّارٍ

Robot إِنسَانٌ آلِيٌّ

A giant **robot.**

إِنسَانٌ آلِيٌّ عِمْلَاقٌ

Roots جُذُورٌ

Plants have **roots** underground.

لِلنَّبَاتَاتِ جُذُورٌ تَحْتَ الأَرْضِ

Ruler مِسْطَرَةٌ/ حَاكِمٌ

The word **ruler** has two meanings.

كَلِمَةُ (رُولَر) بِالإنجِليزِيَّة لَها مَعْنَيان مِسْطَرَة وحَاكِمٌ

Ss

Sandwich سَندَوِيتْشْ

The girl is having a salad **sandwich.**

تَتَنَاوَلُ البِنتُ سَندَوِيتْش سَلَطَةٍ

Scientist عَالِمٌ

Scientists do very clever things.

يَقُومُ العُلَمَاءُ بِأَشْيَاءَ ذَكِيَّةٍ جِدًّا

Sad حَزِينٌ/حَزِينَةٌ

This girl looks so **sad.**

تَبْدُو البِنتُ حَزِينَةً جِدًّا

Sauce صَلْصَةٌ

A bottle of tomato **sauce.**

عُلْبَةُ صَلْصَةِ طَمَاطِمٍ

Scissors مِقَصٌّ

Scissors are used to cut things.

يُسْتَخْدَمُ المِقَصُّ لِقَصِّ الأَشْيَاءِ

Salad سَلَطَةٌ

The girl is having fruit **salad.**

تَتَنَاوَلُ البِنتُ سَلَطَةَ فَوَاكِهَ

Scarf وِشَاحٌ

We wear a **scarf** around our neck.

نَلْبَسُ الوِشَاحَ حَوْلَ رَقَبَتِنَا

Seasons فُصُولٌ

A year has four **seasons.**

فِي السَّنَةِ أَرْبَعَةُ فُصُولٍ

Sand رِمَالٌ

There's a lot of **sand** in the desert.

فِي الصَّحْرَاءِ رِمَالٌ كَثِيرَةٌ

School مَدْرَسَةٌ

At **school** we study.

فِي المَدْرَسَةِ نَدْرُسُ

Shadow ظِلٌّ

Your **shadow** never leaves you.

ظِلُّكَ لَا يُفَارِقُكَ أَبَدًا

Sheep خَرُوفٌ

Some **sheep** like to jump.

بَعْضُ الخِرَافِ تُحِبُّ القَفْزَ

Short قَصِيرٌ

A **short** tree.

شَجَرَةٌ قَصِيرَةٌ

Skyscrapers نَاطِحَاتُ السَّحَاب

Skyscrapers are very tall buildings.

نَاطِحَاتُ السَّحَابِ مَبَانٍ عَالِيَةٌ جِدًّا

Ship سَفِينَةٌ

The **ship** sails on the ocean.

تُبْحِرُ السَّفِينَةُ فِي المُحِيطِ

Sidewalk رَصِيفٌ

A policeman on the **sidewalk**.

شُرْطِيٌّ عَلَى الرَّصِيفِ

Small صَغِيرٌ

A **small** child.

طِفْلٌ صَغِيرٌ

Shirt قَمِيصٌ

A yellow **shirt** is drying.

قَمِيصٌ أَصْفَرُ يَجِفُّ

Skeleton هَيْكَلٌ عَظْمِيٌّ

A dancing **skeleton**.

هَيْكَلٌ عَظْمِيٌّ رَاقِصٌ

Smoke دُخَانٌ

The bird got dirty in the **smoke**.

اتَّسَخَ الطَّيْرُ بِالدُّخَانِ

Shoe حِذَاءٌ

A red **shoe**.

حِذَاء أَحْمَرُ

Sky سَمَاءٌ

The moon, the sun and the **sky**.

القَمَرُ وَالشَّمْسُ وَالسَّمَاءُ

Snail حَلَزُونٌ

The **snail** has a shell on its back.

لِلْحَلَزُونِ صَدَفَةٌ عَلَى ظَهْرِه

Snake أَفْعَى

The **snake** scares the explorer.

تُفْزِعُ الأفْعَى المُسْتَكْشِفَ

Soup شُورْبة

Mmmm…, hot vegetable **soup**.

ممم...، شُورْبَةٌ نَبَاتِيَةٌ سَاخِنَةٌ

Spectacles نَظَّارَاتٌ

What large **spectacles!**

يَا لَهَا مِن نَظَّارَاتٍ كَبِيرَةٍ!

Snowman رَجُلٌ ثَلْجِيٌّ

The **snowman** is feeling cold.

الرَّجُلُ الثَّلْجِيُّ يَشْعُرُ بِالبَرْدِ

South جَنُوبٌ

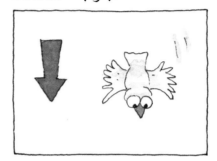

The bird flies towards the **south**.

يَتَّجِهُ الطَّائِرُ نَحْوَ الجَنُوبِ

Spider عَنكَبُوتٌ

The scary **spider** startled Sam.

العَنكَبُوتُ المُرْعِبُ أَذْهَلَ سَامَ

Soap صَابُونٌ

Soap is used for cleaning.

يُستَخْدَمُ الصَّابُونُ لِلتَّنْظِيفِ

Spaceship سَفِينَةُ فَضَاءٍ

A **spaceship** flies to a planet.

سَفِينَةُ الفَضَاءِ تُسَافِرُ إِلَى كَوْكَبٍ

Spoon مِلعَقَةٌ

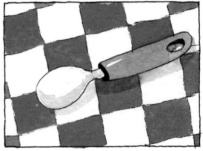

We eat soup with a **spoon**.

نَتَنَاوَلُ الحَسَاءَ بِالمِلْعَقَةِ

Sofa أَرِيكَةٌ

The cat is taking a nap on the **sofa**.

القِطَّةُ تَغْفُو عَلَى الأَرِيكَةِ

Spaghetti مَكَرُونَة اسْبَاجِيتِي

A plateful of yummy **spaghetti**.

صَحْنٌ مَلِئٌ بِمَكرُونَةِ اسْبَاجِيتِي لَذِيذَةٍ

Spring رَبِيعٌ

Spring is fresh and bright.

الرَّبِيعُ مُنْعِشٌ ومُشْرِقٌ

Squirrel سِنْجَابٌ

Squirrels love to crack nuts.

تُحِبُّ السَّنَاجِبُ تَكْسِيرَ الجَوْزِ

Statue تِمْثَالٌ

The statue of a brave cat soldier.

تِمْثَالُ قِطٍّ جُنديٍّ شُجَاعٍ

Summer صَيْفٌ

It gets so hot in summers!

يَشْتَعِلُ الجَوُّ حَرًّا فِي الصَّيْفِ!

Stairs دَرَجٌ

The cat is tiptoeing up the stairs.

تَرْتَقِي القِطَّةُ الدَّرَجَ عَلَى أَطْرَافِ أَصَابِعِها

Stick عَصَا

Blind men walk using a stick.

يَسْتَخْدِمُ الأَعْمَى العَصَا لِلمَشْي

Sun شَمْسٌ

The sun shines during the daytime.

تُشْرِقُ الشَّمْسُ فِي النَّهَارِ

Stamp طَابِعٌ

A stamp from the cat kingdom.

طَابِعٌ مِن مَمْلَكَةِ القِطَطِ

Strawberry فَرَاوْلَةٌ

Mr. and Mrs. Strawberry.

السَّيِّدُ والسَّيِّدَةُ فَرَاوْلَةٌ

Sunflower دَوَّارُ الشَّمْسِ

Sunflowers look towards the sun.

دَوَّارُ الشَّمْسِ يَتَّجِهُ نَحْوَ الشَّمْسِ

Stars نُجُومٌ

Stars come out at night.

تَطْلُعُ النُّجُومُ فِي اللَّيْلِ

Suitcase حَقِيبَةُ سَفَرٍ

It's a very heavy suitcase!

إِنَّها حَقِيبَةُ سَفَرٍ ثَقِيلَةٌ جِدًّا!

Supermarket سُوبَرْ مَارْكِت

Supermarkets have everything.

السُّوبَرْ مَارْكِت فيه كُلُّ شَيْءٍ

Surfboard لَوْحُ رُكُوبِ الأَمْوَاجِ

The boy enjoys his **surfboard.**

يَسْتَمْتِعُ الوَلَدُ بِلَوْحِهِ لِرُكُوبِ الأَمْوَاجِ

Swan إِوَزٌّ

The **swan** prince.

أَمِيرُ الإِوَزِّ

Swing أُرْجُوحَةٌ

The monkey loves his **swing.**

يُحِبُّ القِرْدُ أُرْجُوحَتَهُ

Symbol رَمْزٌ

Math **symbols** puzzle the alien.

تُحَيِّرُ رُمُوزُ الرِّيَاضِيَاتِ المَخْلُوقَ الفَضَائِيَّ

Table طَاوِلَةٌ

The king sits at the **table.**

يَجْلِسُ المَلِكُ عِندَ الطَّاوِلَةِ

Tail ذَيْلٌ

The monkey can swing by his **tail.**

يَسْتَطِيعُ القِرْدُ التَّأَرْجُحَ مُسْتَخْدِمًا ذَيْلَهُ

Tall طَوِيلٌ

A **tall** alien.

مَخْلُوقٌ فَضَائِيٌّ طَوِيلٌ

Taxi تَاكْسِي

A yellow **taxi.**

تَاكْسِي أَصْفَرُ

Teacher مُعَلِّمٌ

A wise **teacher.**

مُعَلِّمٌ حَكِيمٌ

Team فَرِيقٌ

The Cat Kingdom football **team.**

فَرِيقُ كُرَةِ قَدَمِ مَمْلَكَةِ القِطَطِ

Teapot إِبْرِيقُ شَايٍ

A **teapot** is used for serving tea.

يُسْتَخْدَمُ إِبْرِيقُ الشَّايِ لِتَقْدِيمِ الشَّايِ

Telephone هَاتِفٌ

The **telephone** is ringing.

الهَاتِفُ يَرِنُّ

Tiger نَمِرٌ

The **tiger** scares the explorer.

النَّمِرُ يُخِيفُ المُسْتَكْشِفَ

Toothbrush فُرْشَاةُ أَسْنَانٍ

The cat is using a red **toothbrush**.

تَسْتَعْمِلُ القِطَّةُ فُرْشَاةَ أَسْنَانٍ حَمْرَاءَ

Television تِلِفِزْيُونٌ

The cat is watching **television**.

تُشَاهِدُ القِطَّةُ التِلِفِزْيُونَ

Time وَقْتٌ

Can you tell what **time** is it?

هَل لَكَ أَن تُخْبِرَنِي بِالوَقْتِ رَجَاءً؟

Top خُذْرُوفٌ

A **top** is a toy that spins.

الخُذْرُوفُ لُعْبَةٌ تَدُورُ

Tent خَيْمَةٌ

The colourful circus **tents**.

خِيَامُ السِّيرْكِ المُلَوَّنَةِ

Tissue مَنْدِيلٌ وَرَقِيٌّ

We use a **tissue** while sneezing.

نَسْتَعْمِلُ مَنْدِيلاً وَرَقِيّاً عِندَ العَطْسِ

Torch كَشَّافٌ

The cat with a **torch**.

القِطَّةُ مَعَهَا كَشَّافٌ

Ticket تَذْكِرَةٌ

I have a **ticket** to the circus!

عِندِي تَذْكِرَةٌ لِلسِّيرْكِ

Tomato طَمَاطِمٌ

We make ketchup from **tomatoes**.

نَصْنَعُ الكَاتْشِبَ مِن الطَّمَاطِمِ

Towel مِنْشَفَةٌ

The boy in his bath **towel**.

الوَلَدُ مُلَتَّفٌ بِمِنْشَفَةِ الحَمَّامِ

Toy لُعْبَة

A couple of cuddly soft **toys**.

زَوْجٌ مِن اللُّعَبِ النَّاعِمَةِ المَحْبُوبَةِ

Trash can صُنْدُوقُ قُمَامَةٍ

The **trash can** is full of garbage.

صُنْدُوقُ القُمَامَةِ مَلِيءٌ بِالقُمَامَةِ

Tractor تَرَكْتَرٌ

The cat is driving a red **tractor**.

القِطَّةُ تَقُودُ تَرَكْتَرًا أَحْمَرَ

Tree شَجَرَةٌ

A multi-storied **tree**.

شَجَرَةٌ مُتَعَدِّدَةُ الطَّوابِقِ

Umbrella شَمْسِيَّةٌ

A big beach **umbrella**.

شَمْسِيَّةُ شَاطِئٍ كَبِيرَةٌ

Traffic light إِشَارَةُ مُرُورٍ

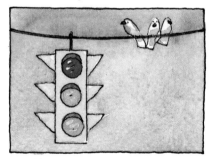

Traffic lights are very useful.

إِشَارَاتُ المُرُورِ مُفِيدَةٌ جِدًّا

Trunk خُرْطُومٌ

The elephant's **trunk** is long.

خُرْطُومُ الفِيلِ طَوِيلٌ

Uncle عَمٌّ

My **uncle** has a long moustache.

لِعَمِّي شَارِب طَوِيل

Train قِطَارٌ

The engine pulls the **train**.

يَجُرُّ المُحَرِّكُ القِطَارَ

Tunnel نَفَقٌ

It can be dark in a **tunnel**.

قَدْ يَكُونُ النَّفَقُ مُظْلِماً

Underground جَوْفُ الأَرْضِ

Rabbits live **underground**.

تَعِيشُ الأَرَانِبُ في جَوْفِ الأَرْضِ

Unicorn يونِيكورن

This is a **unicorn**.

هَذَا يونِيكورن

Uniform زِيٌّ رَسْمِيٌّ

This is our school **uniform**.

هَذَا زِيُّ مَدْرَسَتِنَا الرَّسْمِيُّ

Universe كَوْنٌ

The **universe** is so vast.

الكَوْنُ وَاسِعٌ جِدًّا

Upside down رَأْسًا عَلَى عَقِبٍ

The boy is swinging **upside down**.

يَتَأَرْجَحُ الوَلَدُ رَأْسًا عَلَى عَقِبٍ

Vase مِزْهَرِيَّةٌ

The naughty cat pushed the **vase**.

دَفَعَتِ القِطَّةُ المُزْعِجَةُ المِزْهَرِيَّةَ

Vacuum cleaner مِكْنَسَةٌ كَهْرَبائِيَّة

Cleaning with a **vacuum cleaner**.

التَّنْظِيفُ بِمِكْنَسَةٍ كَهْرَبائِيَّةٍ

Valley وَادِي

A beautiful view of a **valley**.

مَنظَرُ وَادٍ جَمِيلٍ

Van عَرَبَةٌ

A mouse trap **van**.

شَرَكُ فَأْرٍ فِي شَكْلِ عَرَبَةٍ

Vegetable خُضْرَوَاتٌ

Vegetables are good for health.

الخُضْرَوَاتُ مُفِيدَةٌ لِلصِّحَّةِ

View إِطْلالَةٌ

A nice **view** from the balloon.

إِطْلالَةٌ جَمِيلَةٌ مِن المِنطادِ

Village قَرْيَةٌ

An African **village**.

قَرْيَةٌ أَفْرِيقِيَّةٌ

Washing machine غَسَّالَةُ مَلابِسَ

A big **washing machine**.
غَسَّالَةُ مَلابِسَ كَبِيرَةٌ

Wave مَوْجَةٌ

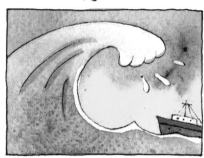

A giant **wave**.
مَوْجَةٌ عِمْلاقَةٌ

Wall جِدارٌ

A **wall** is hard to climb.
تَسَلُّقُ الجِدارِ صَعْبٌ

Wasp دَبُّورٌ

A **wasp** sting is painful.
لَدْغَةُ الدَّبُّورِ مُؤْلِمَةٌ

Weather طَقْسٌ

The **weather** is very hot now.
الطَّقْسُ حارٌّ جِدًّا الآنَ

Wallet مِحْفَظَةٌ

The fox dropped his **wallet**.
أَسْقَطَ الثَّعْلَبُ مِحْفَظَتَهُ

Watch ساعَةُ يَدٍ

A teddy bear **watch**.
ساعَةُ يَدٍ فِي شَكْلِ دُبٍّ

Web شَبَكَةٌ

The spider weaves a **web**.
يَنْسِجُ العَنْكَبُوتُ شَبَكَةً

Wardrobe خِزانَةُ مَلابِسَ

A blue **wardrobe**.
خِزانَةُ مَلابِسَ زَرْقاءُ

Waterfall شَلّالٌ

The **waterfall** has a terrible flow!
لِلشَّلّالِ تَدَفُّقٌ رَهِيبٌ!

Website مَوْقِعُ الشَّبَكَةِ

The cat is surfing the **website**.
تَتَصَفَّحُ القِطَّةُ مَوْقِعَ الشَّبَكَةِ

West غَرْبٌ

The bird is flying towards the **west**.

الطَّائِرُ مُتَّجِهٌ نَحْوَ الغَرْبِ

Whisker شَارِبٌ

The cat has long **whiskers**.

لِلْقِطَّةِ شَوَارِبُ طَوِيلَةٌ

Window نَافِذَةٌ

A boy stands at a **window**.

يَقِفُ الوَلَدُ جِوَارَ نَافِذَةٍ

Wet مُبْتَلٌّ

In rain we get **wet**.

المَطَرُ يُبَلِّلُنَا

Wild بَرِّي / بَرِّيَّة

Wild animals live in the jungle.

تَعِيشُ الحَيَوَانَاتُ البَرِّيَّةُ فِي الغَابَةِ

Wing جَنَاحٌ

An eagle has long **wings**.

لِلنَّسْرِ أَجْنِحَةٌ طَوِيلَةٌ

Whale حُوتٌ

The **whale** is the biggest creature.

الحُوتُ أَكْبَرُ المَخْلُوقَاتِ

Wind رِيَاحٌ

The **wind** is blowing hard.

تَهُبُّ الرِّيَاحُ بِشِدَّةٍ

Winter شِتَاءٌ

It can be very cold in **winter**.

قَدْ يَكُونُ الطَّقْسُ قَارِصًا فِي الشِّتَاءِ

Wheelbarrow عَرَبَةُ يَدٍ

A **wheelbarrow** full of leaves.

عَرَبَةُ يَدٍ مَلِيئَةٌ بِوَرَقِ الشَّجَرِ

Windmill طَاحُونَةٌ هَوَائِيَّةٌ

The wind moves **windmills**.

تُحَرِّكُ الرِّيَاحُ الطَّوَاحِينَ الهَوَائِيَّةَ

Wolf ذِئْبٌ

The **wolf** and the Red Riding Hood.

الذِّئْبُ وَذَاتُ الرِّدَاءِ الأَحْمَرِ

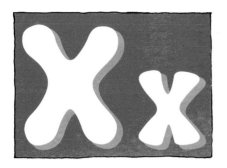

X-mas الكِرِيسْمَاس

Xmas is a time for good cheer.

الكِرِيسْمَاسُ وَقْتٌ لِلمَرَحِ الجَمِيلِ

Yacht يَخْتٌ

The cat is sailing on a **yacht.**

تُبْحِرُ القِطَّةُ عَلَى يَخْتٍ

Zebra حِمَارٌ وَحْشِيٌّ

The **zebra** has stripes like a tiger.

لِلْحِمَارِ الوَحْشِيِّ خُطُوطٌ كَخُطُوطِ النَّمِر

X-ray أَشِعَّةٌ سِينِيَّةٌ

The **x-rays** scan our bones.

تُصَوِّرُ الأَشِعَّةُ السِّينِيَّةُ عِظَامَنَا

Yellow أَصْفَر

All these things are **yellow** in color.

كُلُّ هَذِهِ الأَشْيَاءِ صَفْرَاءُ اللَوْنِ

Zip سُسْتَةٌ

A blue jacket with a yellow **zip.**

سُتْرَةٌ زَرْقَاءُ بِسُسْتَةٍ صَفْرَاء

Xylophone زيلفون

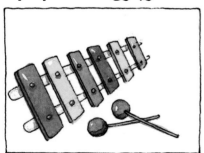

The **xylophone** is tuneful.

الزيلفون جَمِيلُ الصَّوْتِ

Yolk مُحٌّ

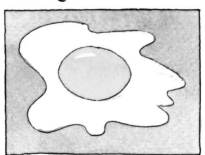

Yolk is the yellow of the egg.

المُحُّ صَفَارُ البَيْضِ

Zoo حَدِيقَةُ حَيَوَانَاتٍ

Wild animals in the **zoo.**

حَيَوَانَاتٌ بَرِّيَّةٌ فِي حَدِيقَةِ الحَيَوَانَاتِ